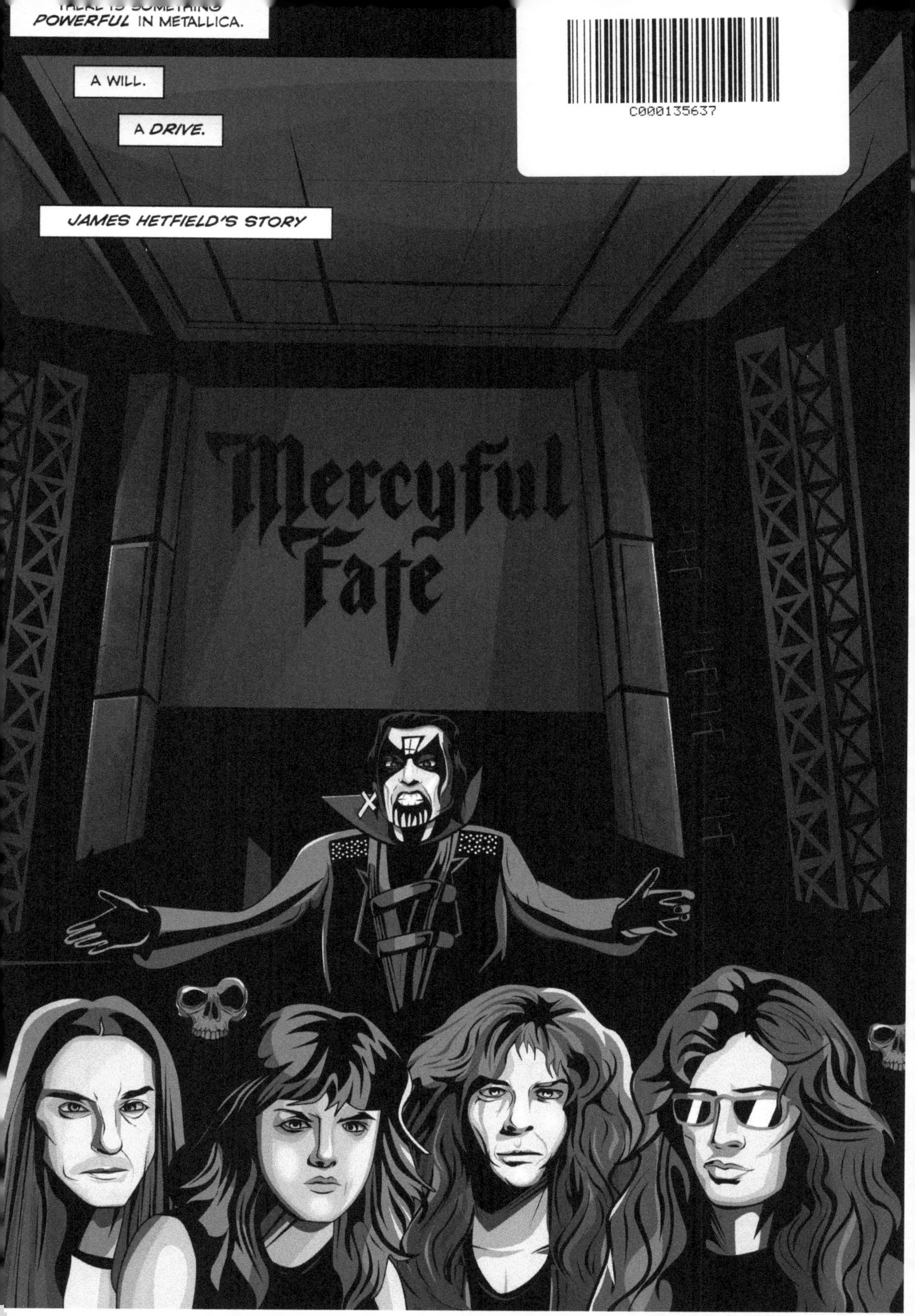
POWERFUL IN METALLICA.
A WILL.
A DRIVE.
JAMES HETFIELD'S STORY
Mercyful Fate

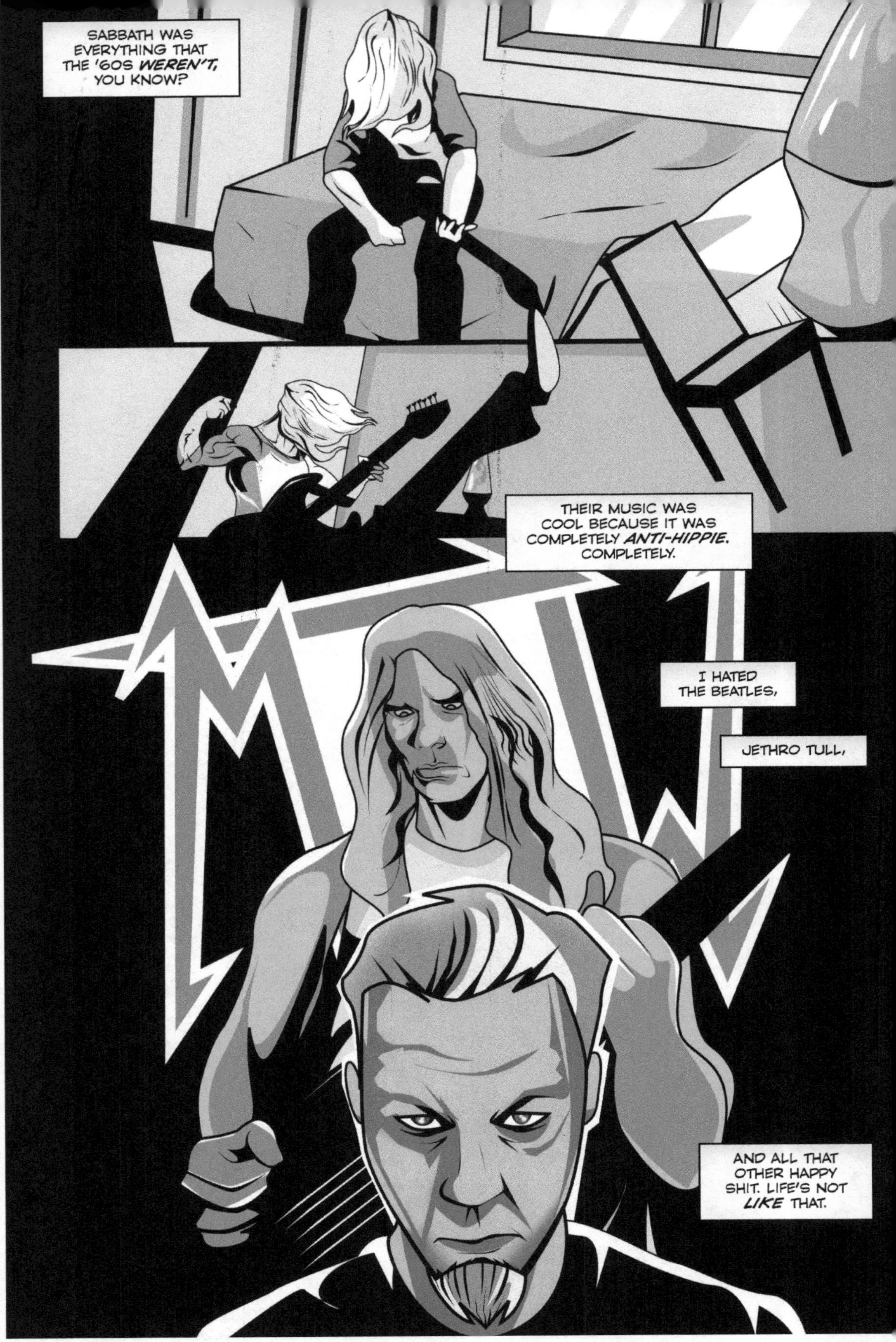
SABBATH WAS EVERYTHING THAT THE '60S WEREN'T, YOU KNOW?
THEIR MUSIC WAS COOL BECAUSE IT WAS COMPLETELY ANTI-HIPPIE. COMPLETELY.
I HATED THE BEATLES,
JETHRO TULL,
AND ALL THAT OTHER HAPPY SHIT. LIFE'S NOT LIKE THAT.

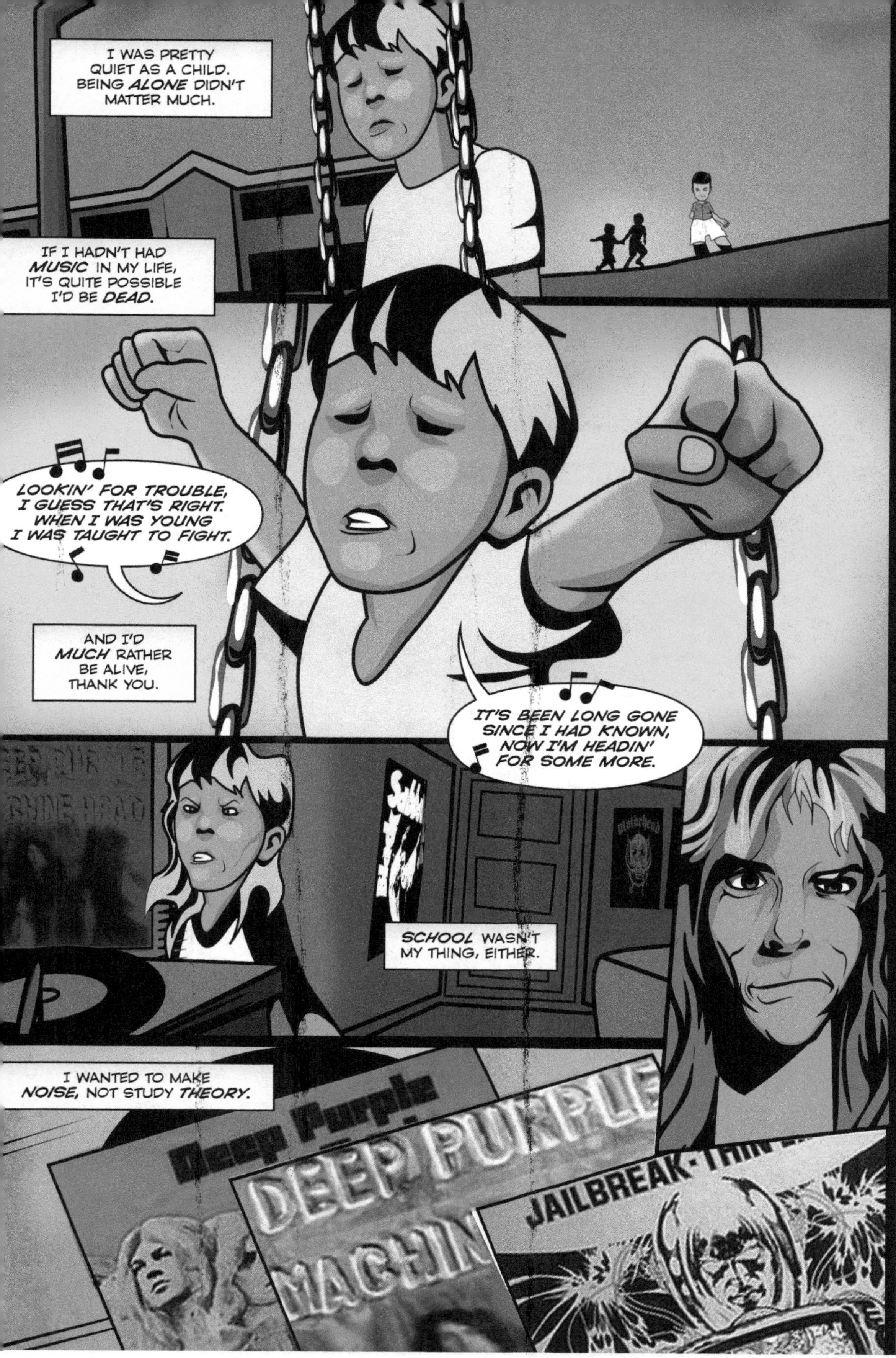

I WAS PRETTY QUIET AS A CHILD. BEING ALONE DIDN'T MATTER MUCH.
IF I HADN'T HAD MUSIC IN MY LIFE, IT'S QUITE POSSIBLE I'D BE DEAD.
LOOKIN' FOR TROUBLE, I GUESS THAT'S RIGHT. WHEN I WAS YOUNG I WAS TAUGHT TO FIGHT.
AND I'D MUCH RATHER BE ALIVE, THANK YOU.
IT'S BEEN LONG GONE SINCE I HAD KNOWN, NOW I'M HEADIN' FOR SOME MORE.
SCHOOL WASN'T MY THING, EITHER.
I WANTED TO MAKE NOISE, NOT STUDY THEORY.
Deep Purple
DEEP PURPLE
MACHIN
JAILBREAK

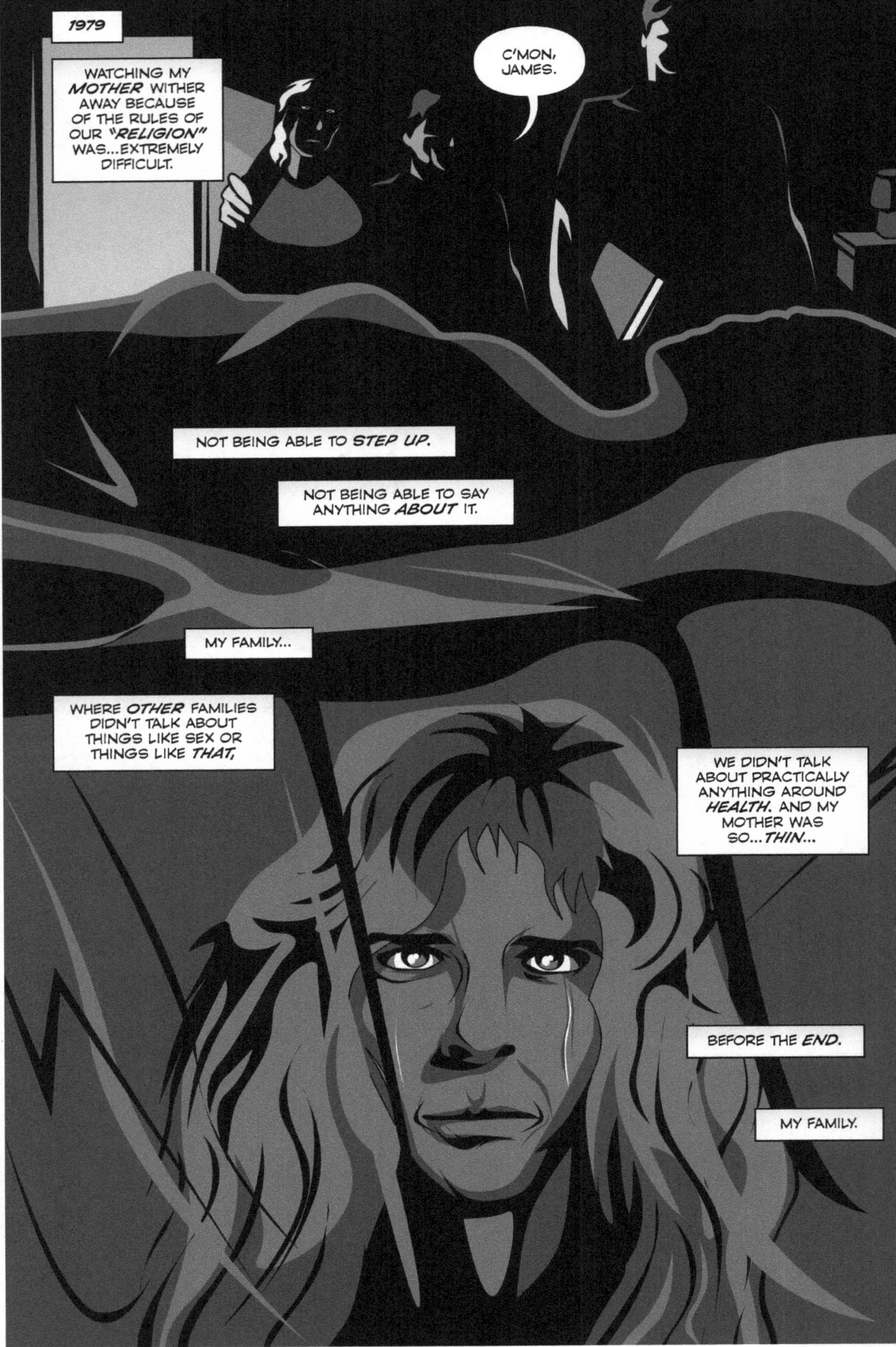
1979
WATCHING MY MOTHER WITHER AWAY BECAUSE OF THE RULES OF OUR "RELIGION" WAS...EXTREMELY DIFFICULT.
C'MON, JAMES.
NOT BEING ABLE TO STEP UP.
NOT BEING ABLE TO SAY ANYTHING ABOUT IT.
MY FAMILY...
WHERE OTHER FAMILIES DIDN'T TALK ABOUT THINGS LIKE SEX OR THINGS LIKE THAT,
WE DIDN'T TALK ABOUT PRACTICALLY ANYTHING AROUND HEALTH. AND MY MOTHER WAS SO...THIN...
BEFORE THE END.
MY FAMILY.

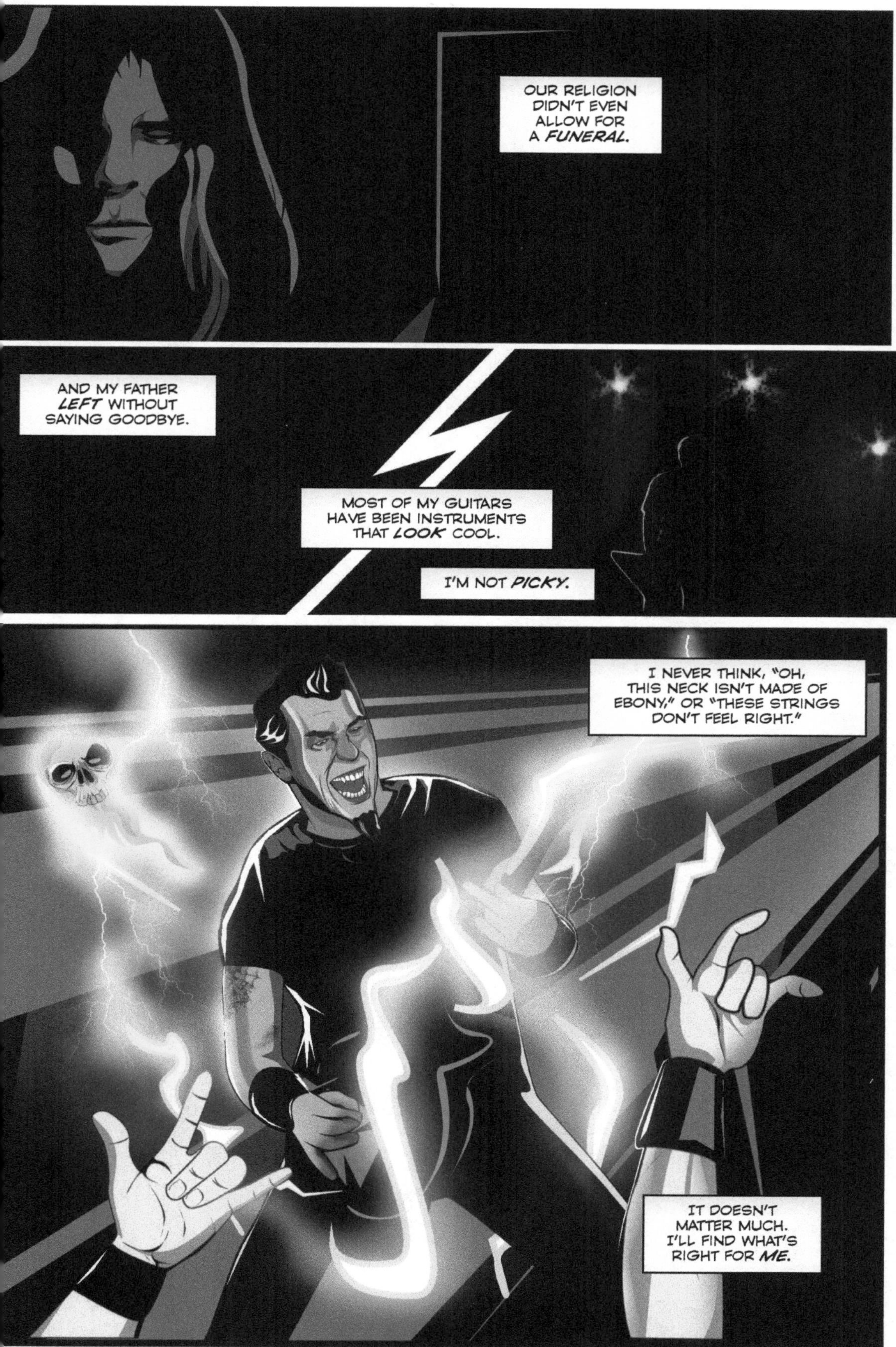
OUR RELIGION DIDN'T EVEN ALLOW FOR A FUNERAL.
AND MY FATHER LEFT WITHOUT SAYING GOODBYE.
MOST OF MY GUITARS HAVE BEEN INSTRUMENTS THAT LOOK COOL.
I'M NOT PICKY.
I NEVER THINK, "OH, THIS NECK ISN'T MADE OF EBONY," OR "THESE STRINGS DON'T FEEL RIGHT."
IT DOESN'T MATTER MUCH. I'LL FIND WHAT'S RIGHT FOR ME.

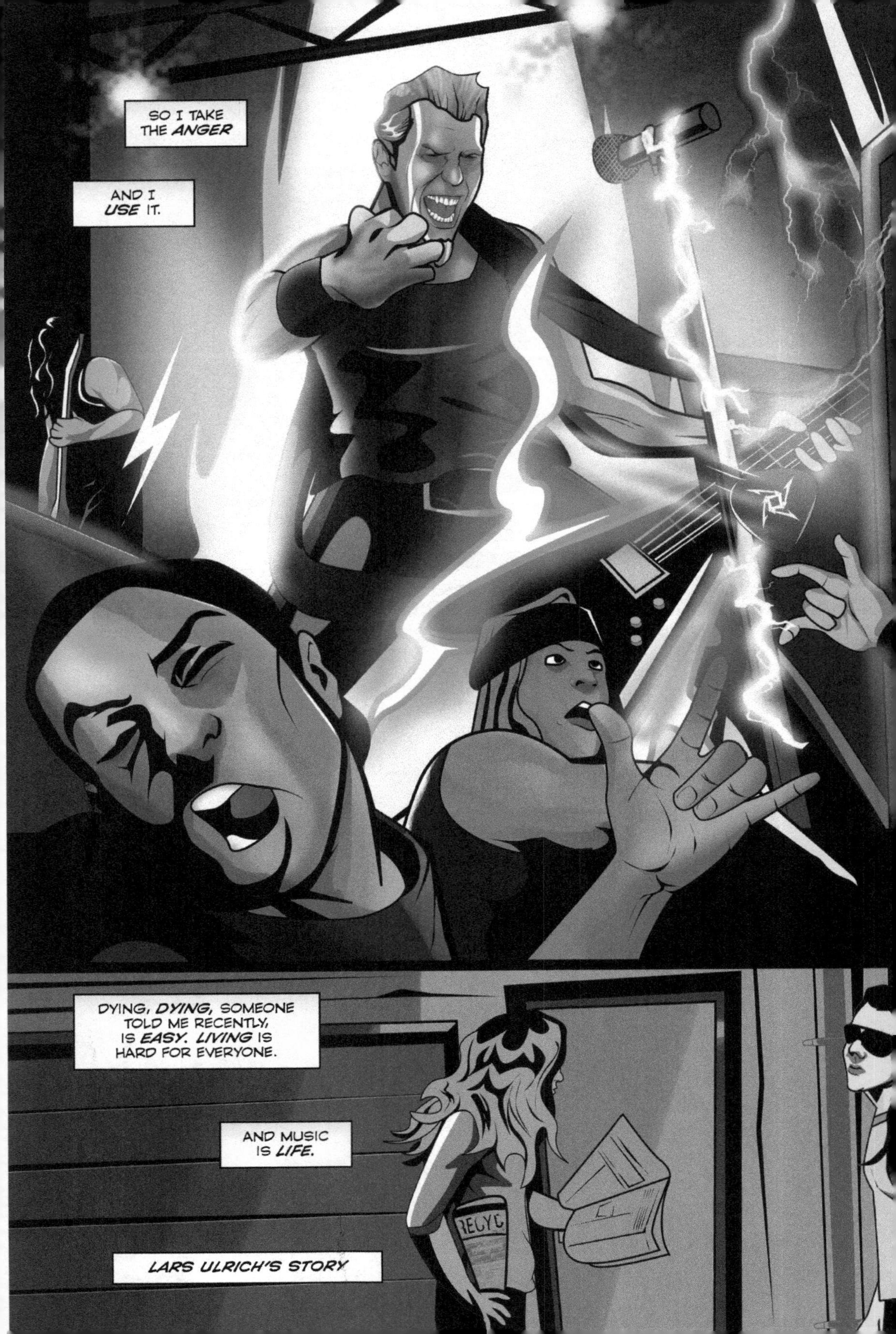
SO I TAKE THE *ANGER*
AND I *USE* IT.
DYING, *DYING*, SOMEONE TOLD ME RECENTLY, IS *EASY*. *LIVING* IS HARD FOR EVERYONE.
AND MUSIC IS *LIFE*.
LARS ULRICH'S STORY

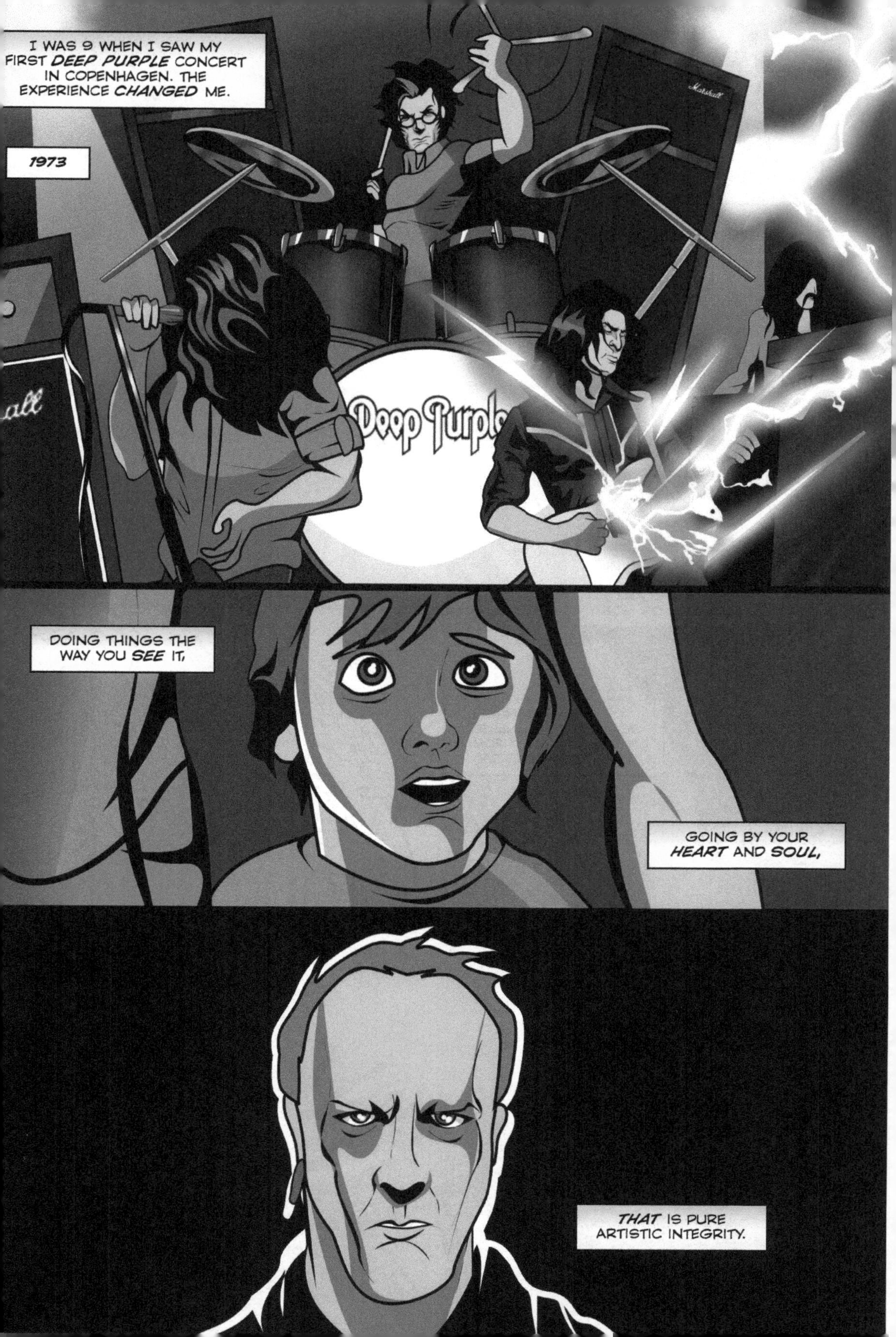
I WAS 9 WHEN I SAW MY FIRST *DEEP PURPLE* CONCERT IN COPENHAGEN. THE EXPERIENCE *CHANGED* ME.
1973
Marshall
Deep Purple
DOING THINGS THE WAY YOU *SEE* IT,
GOING BY YOUR *HEART* AND *SOUL*,
THAT IS PURE ARTISTIC INTEGRITY.

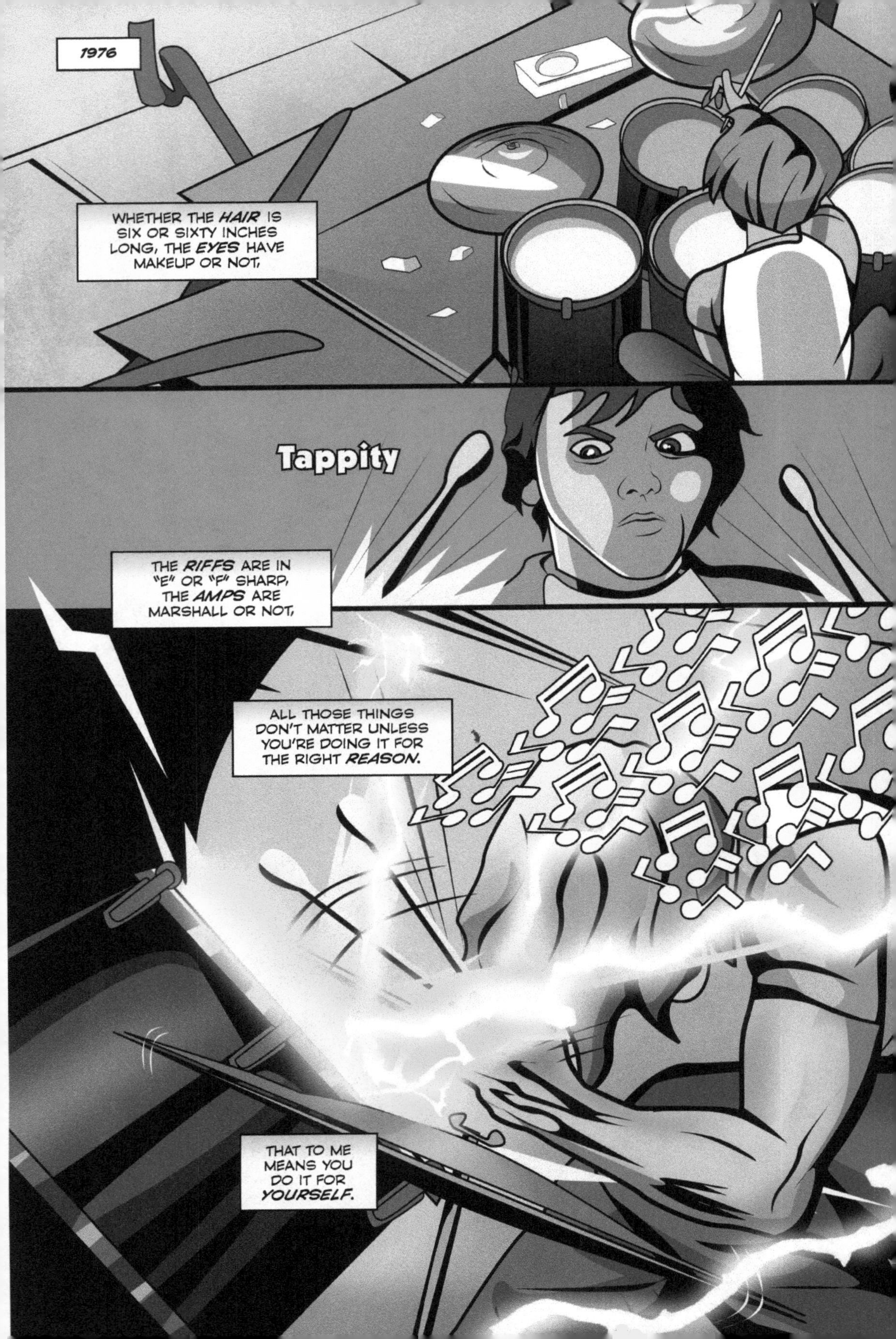
1976
WHETHER THE *HAIR* IS SIX OR SIXTY INCHES LONG, THE *EYES* HAVE MAKEUP OR NOT,
Tappity
THE *RIFFS* ARE IN "E" OR "F" SHARP, THE *AMPS* ARE MARSHALL OR NOT,
ALL THOSE THINGS DON'T MATTER UNLESS YOU'RE DOING IT FOR THE RIGHT *REASON*.
THAT TO ME MEANS YOU DO IT FOR *YOURSELF*.

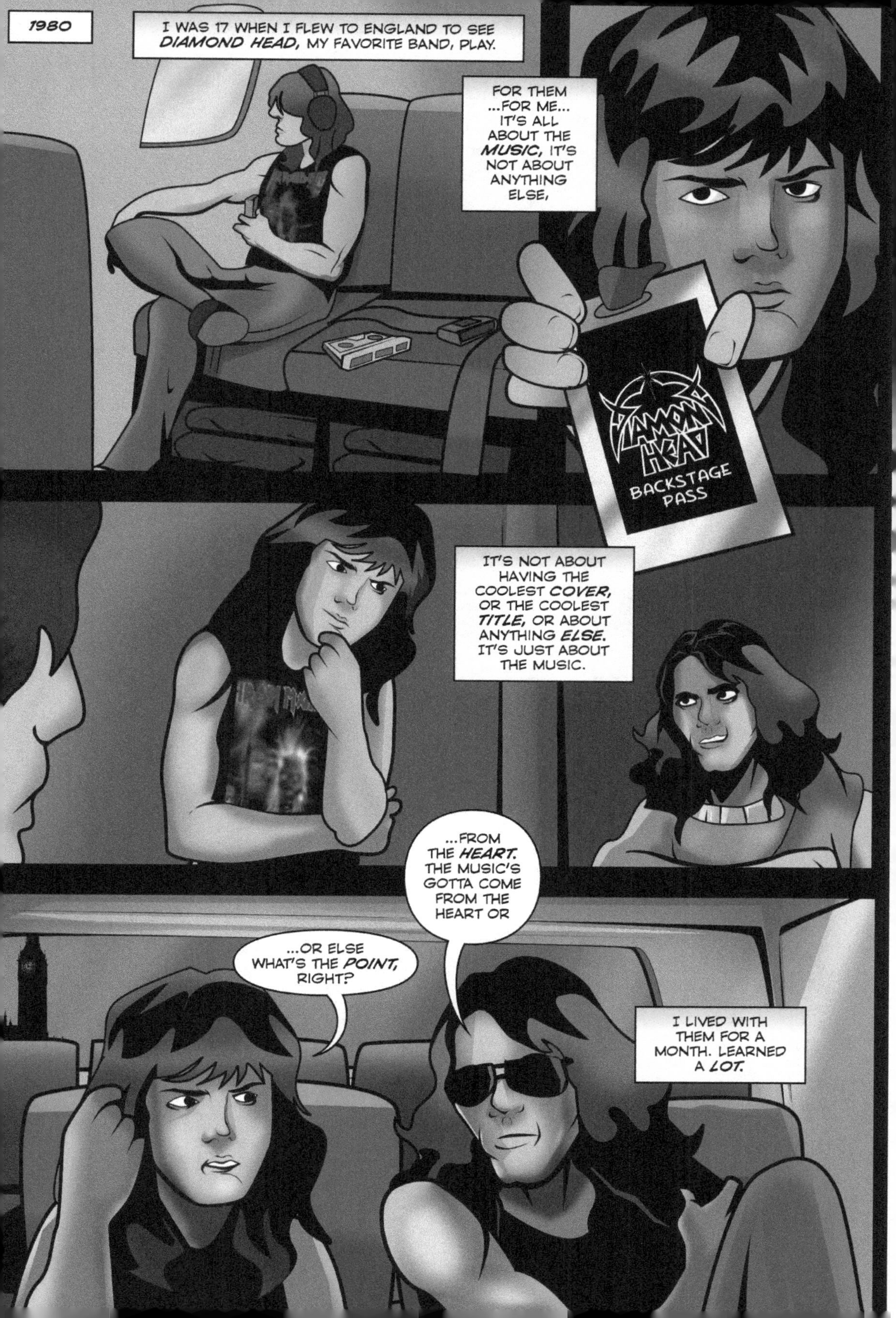
1980
I WAS 17 WHEN I FLEW TO ENGLAND TO SEE DIAMOND HEAD, MY FAVORITE BAND, PLAY.
FOR THEM ...FOR ME... IT'S ALL ABOUT THE MUSIC, IT'S NOT ABOUT ANYTHING ELSE,
DIAMOND HEAD BACKSTAGE PASS
IT'S NOT ABOUT HAVING THE COOLEST COVER, OR THE COOLEST TITLE, OR ABOUT ANYTHING ELSE. IT'S JUST ABOUT THE MUSIC.
...FROM THE HEART. THE MUSIC'S GOTTA COME FROM THE HEART OR
...OR ELSE WHAT'S THE POINT, RIGHT?
I LIVED WITH THEM FOR A MONTH. LEARNED A LOT.

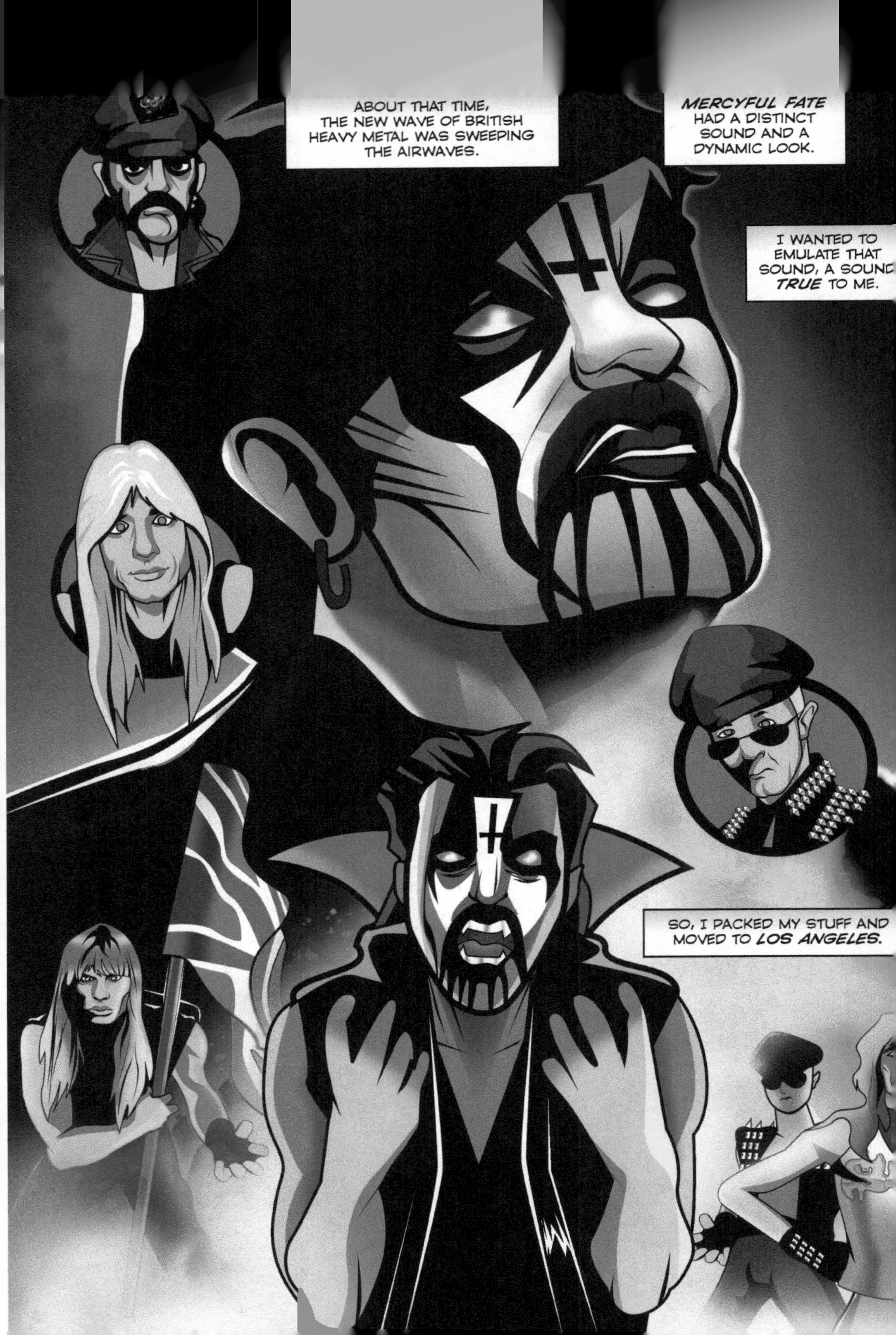
ABOUT THAT TIME, THE NEW WAVE OF BRITISH HEAVY METAL WAS SWEEPING THE AIRWAVES.
MERCYFUL FATE HAD A DISTINCT SOUND AND A DYNAMIC LOOK.
I WANTED TO EMULATE THAT SOUND, A SOUND TRUE TO ME.
SO, I PACKED MY STUFF AND MOVED TO LOS ANGELES.

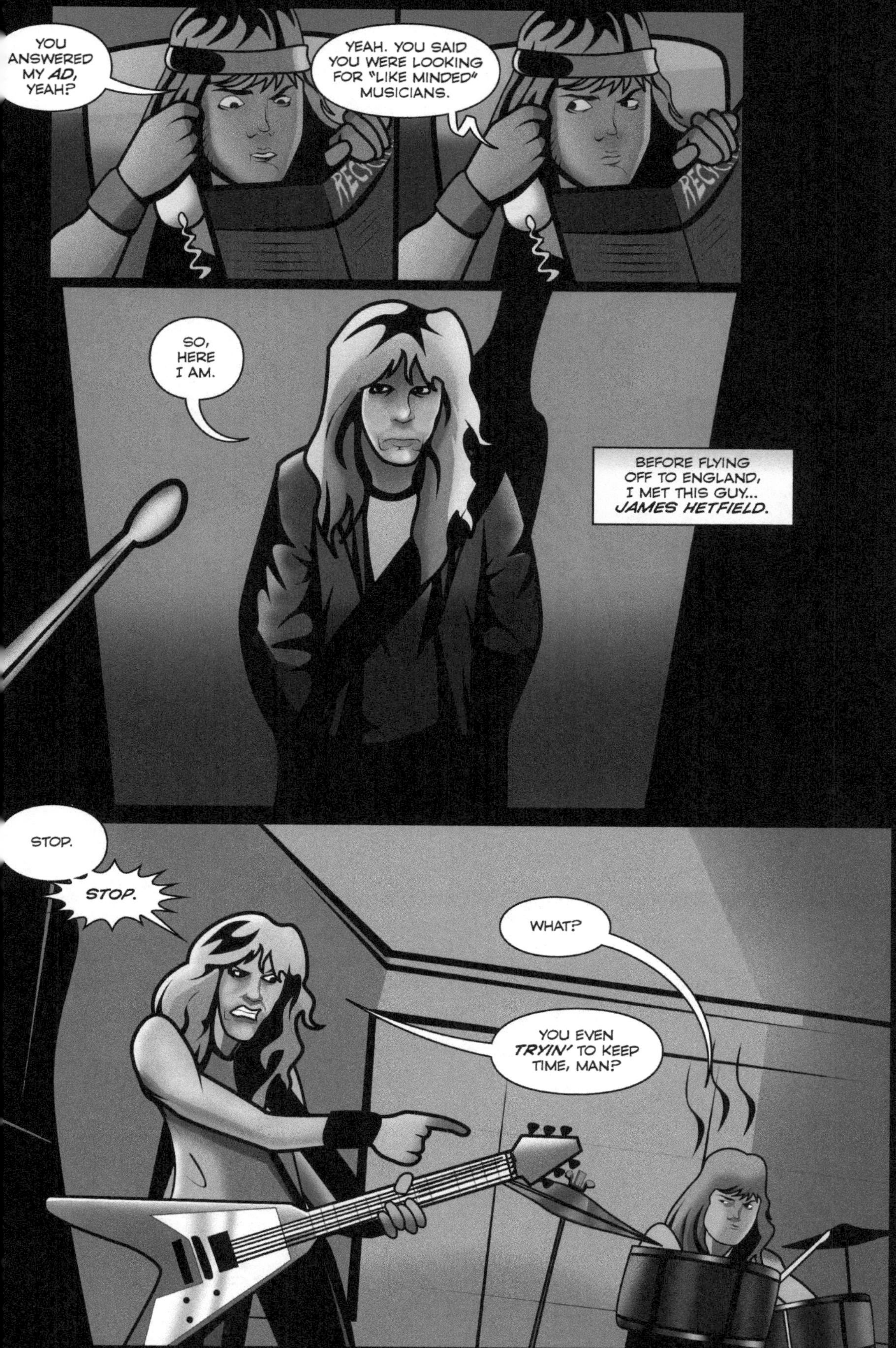
YOU ANSWERED MY AD, YEAH?
YEAH. YOU SAID YOU WERE LOOKING FOR "LIKE MINDED" MUSICIANS.
SO, HERE I AM.
BEFORE FLYING OFF TO ENGLAND, I MET THIS GUY... JAMES HETFIELD.
STOP.
STOP.
WHAT?
YOU EVEN TRYIN' TO KEEP TIME, MAN?

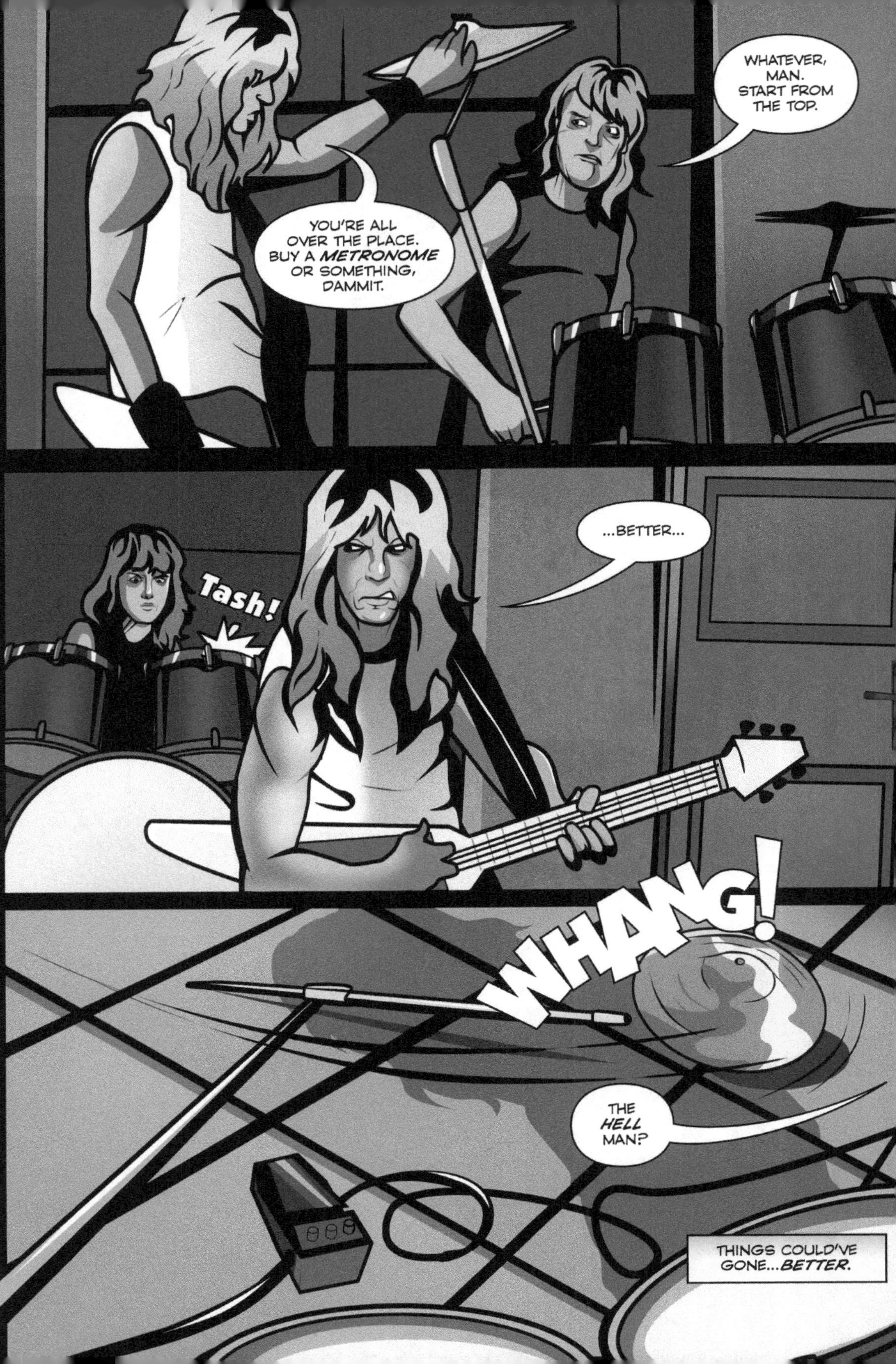
WHATEVER, MAN. START FROM THE TOP.
YOU'RE ALL OVER THE PLACE. BUY A *METRONOME* OR SOMETHING, DAMMIT.
Tash!
...BETTER...
WHANG!
THE *HELL* MAN?
THINGS COULD'VE GONE... *BETTER.*

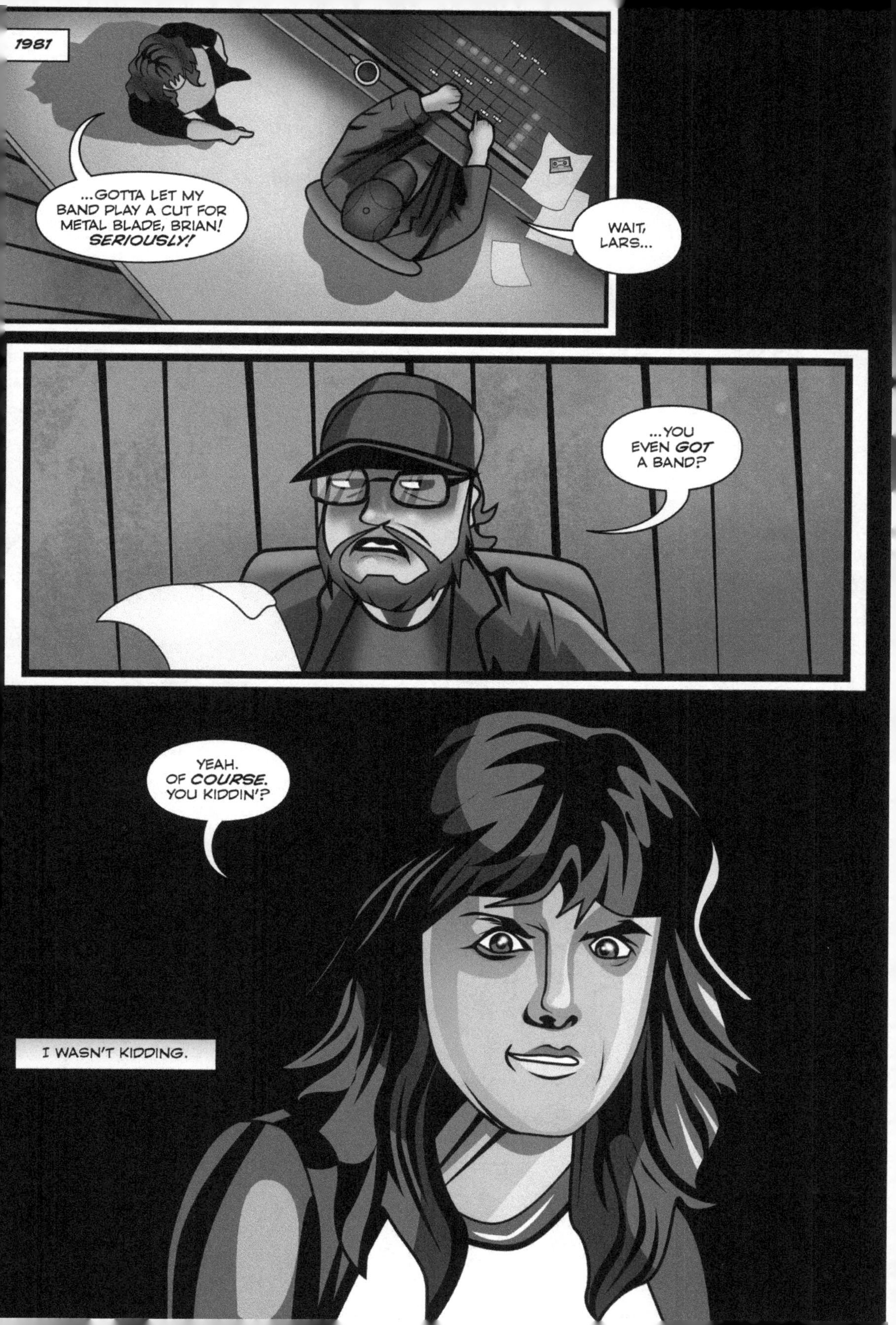
1981
...GOTTA LET MY BAND PLAY A CUT FOR METAL BLADE, BRIAN! SERIOUSLY!
WAIT, LARS...
...YOU EVEN GOT A BAND?
YEAH. OF COURSE. YOU KIDDIN'?
I WASN'T KIDDING.

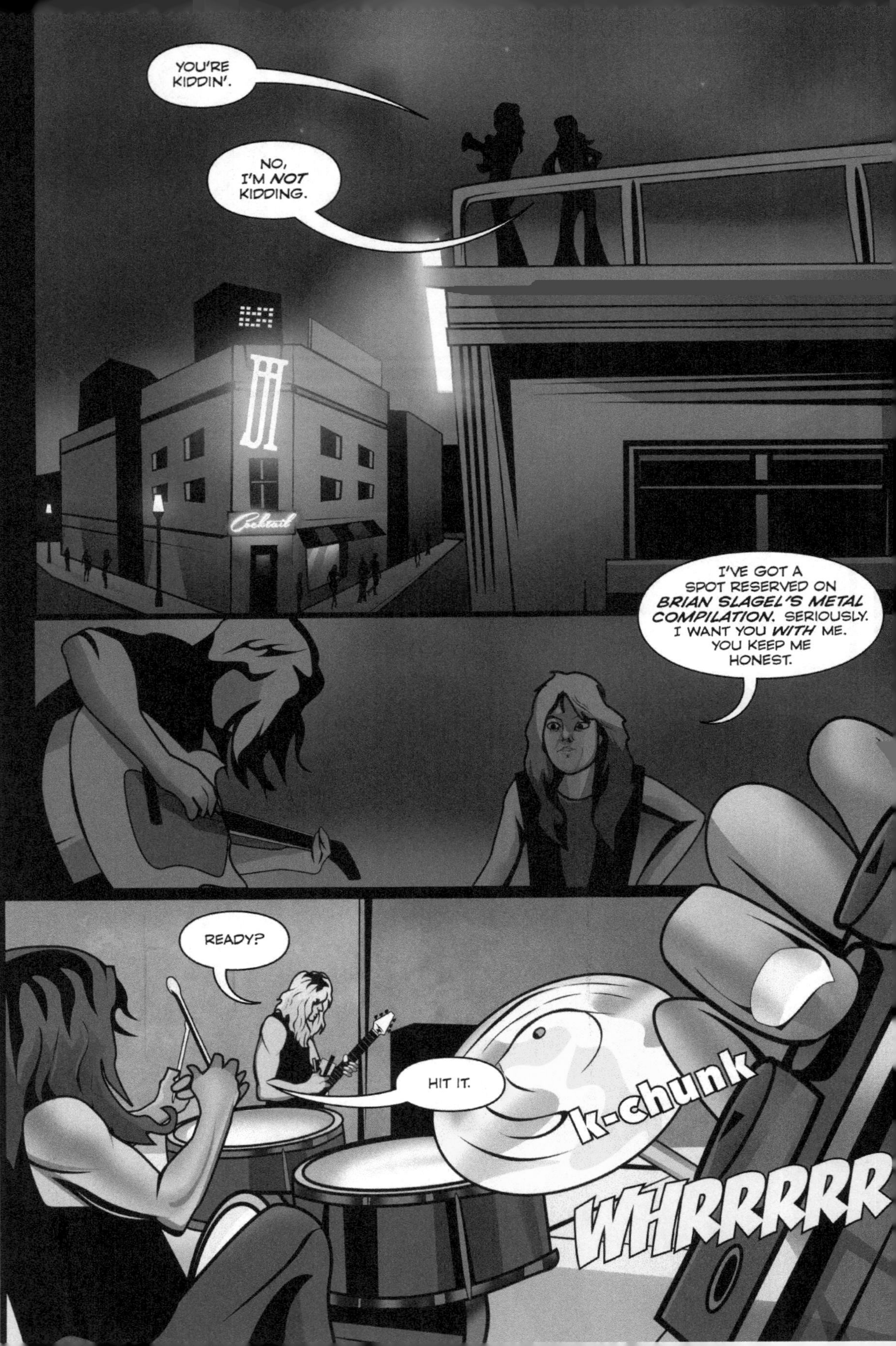
YOU'RE KIDDIN'.
NO, I'M *NOT* KIDDING.
Cocktail
I'VE GOT A SPOT RESERVED ON ***BRIAN SLAGEL'S METAL COMPILATION.*** SERIOUSLY. I WANT YOU *WITH* ME. YOU KEEP ME HONEST.
READY?
HIT IT.
k-chunk
WHRRRRR

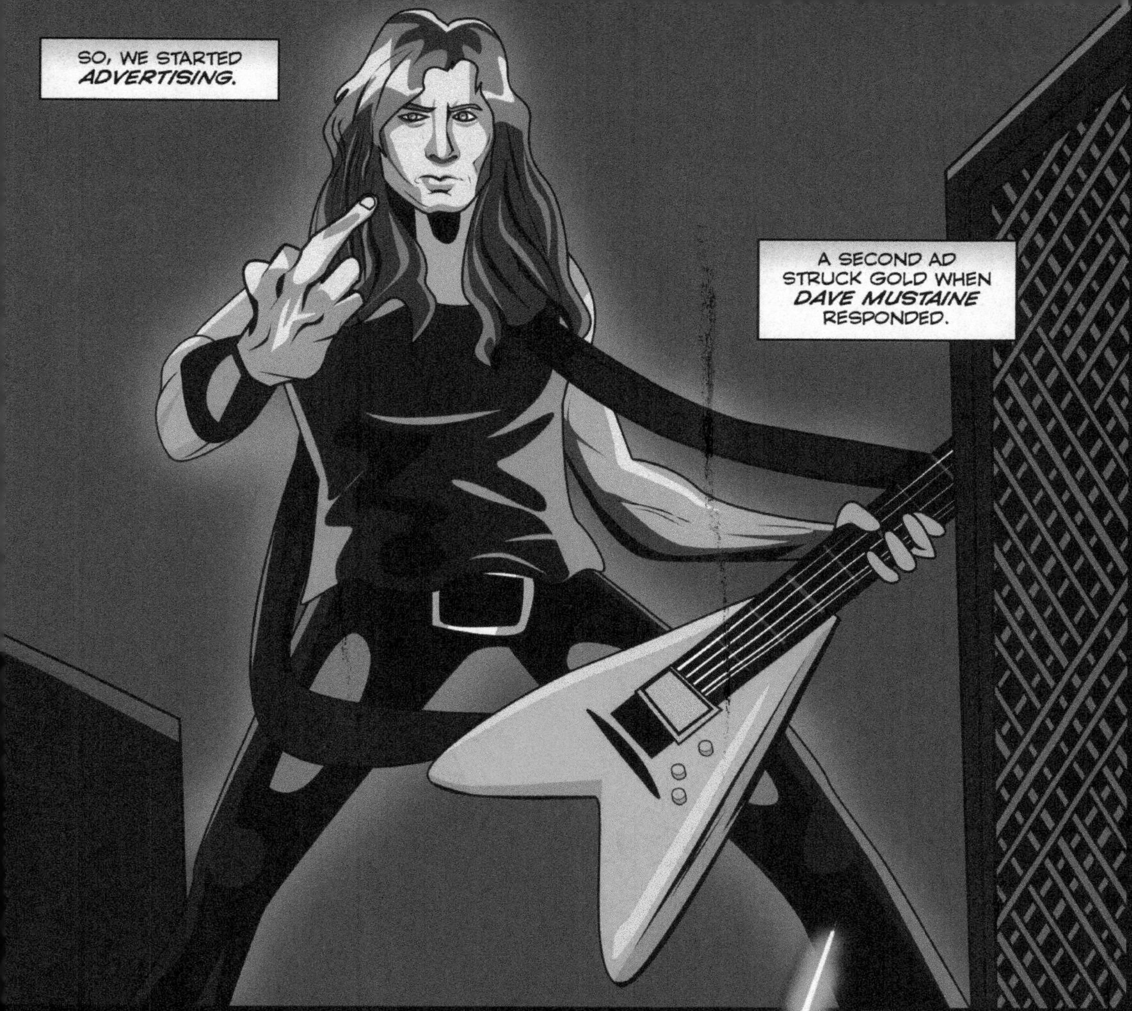
SO, WE STARTED *ADVERTISING.*
A SECOND AD STRUCK GOLD WHEN ***DAVE MUSTAINE*** RESPONDED.

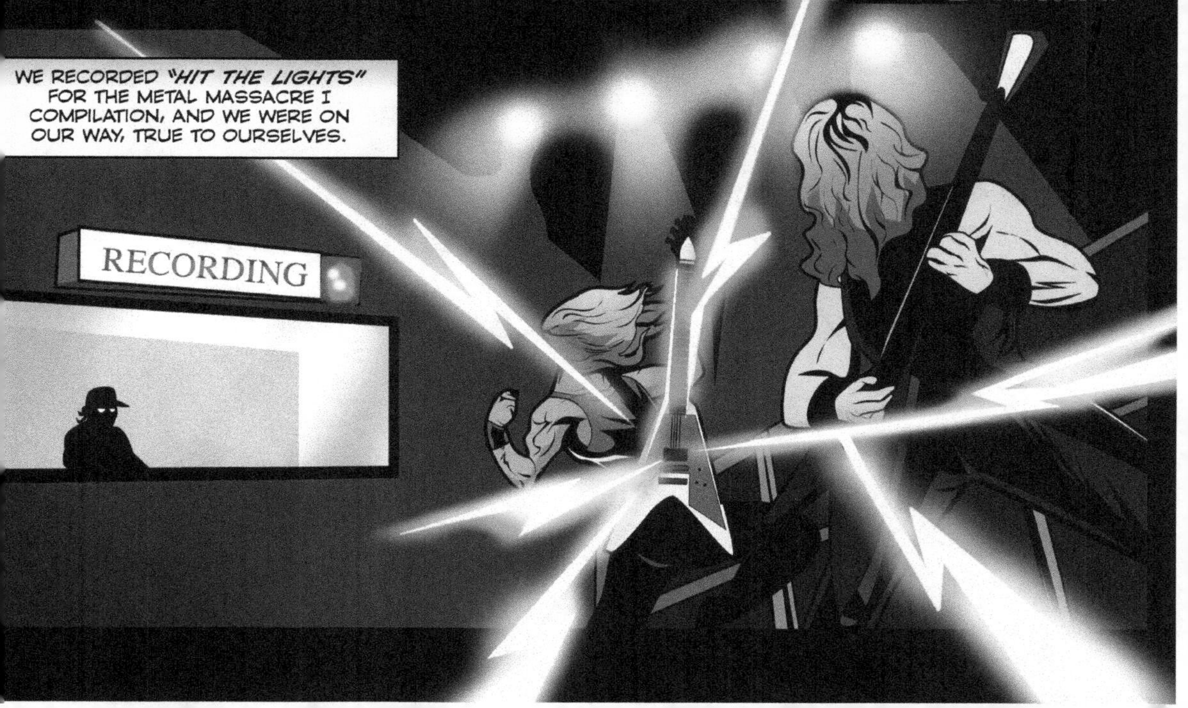
WE RECORDED *"HIT THE LIGHTS"* FOR THE METAL MASSACRE I COMPILATION, AND WE WERE ON OUR WAY, TRUE TO OURSELVES.
RECORDING

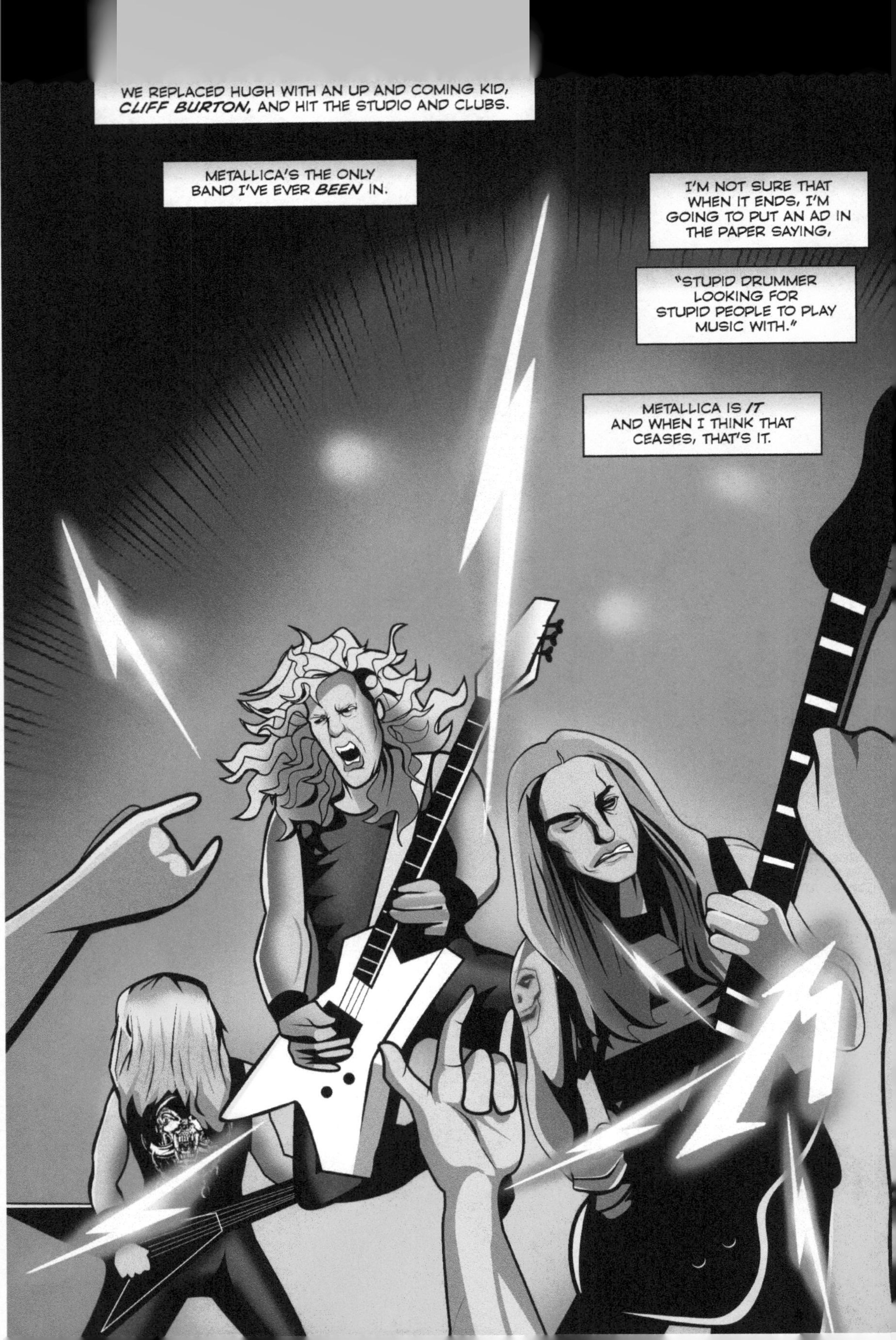
WE REPLACED HUGH WITH AN UP AND COMING KID, *CLIFF BURTON,* AND HIT THE STUDIO AND CLUBS.
METALLICA'S THE ONLY BAND I'VE EVER *BEEN* IN.
I'M NOT SURE THAT WHEN IT ENDS, I'M GOING TO PUT AN AD IN THE PAPER SAYING,
"STUPID DRUMMER LOOKING FOR STUPID PEOPLE TO PLAY MUSIC WITH."
METALLICA IS *IT* AND WHEN I THINK THAT CEASES, THAT'S IT.

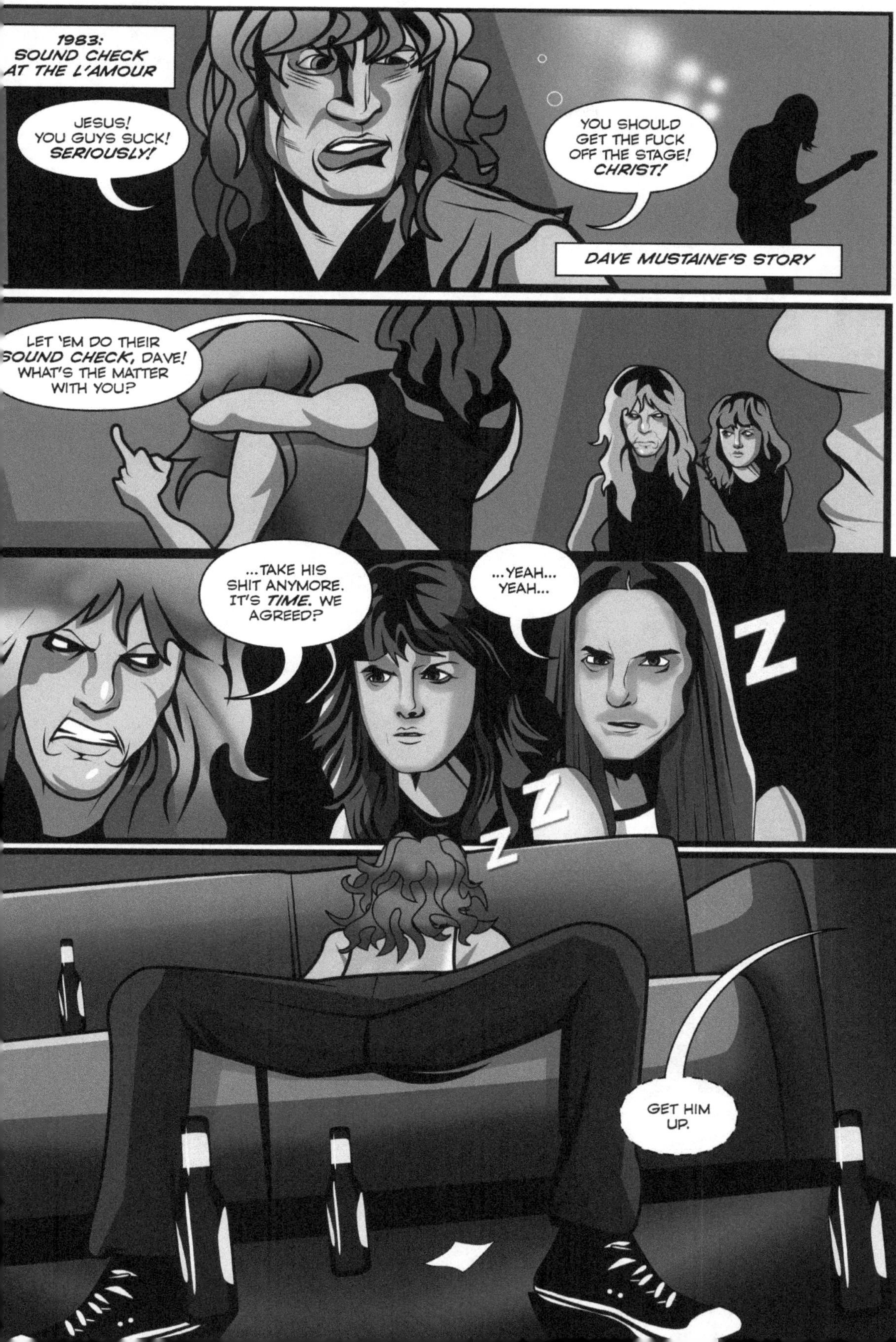
1983:
SOUND CHECK
AT THE L'AMOUR
JESUS! YOU GUYS SUCK! SERIOUSLY!
YOU SHOULD GET THE FUCK OFF THE STAGE! CHRIST!
DAVE MUSTAINE'S STORY
LET 'EM DO THEIR SOUND CHECK, DAVE! WHAT'S THE MATTER WITH YOU?
...TAKE HIS SHIT ANYMORE. IT'S TIME. WE AGREED?
...YEAH... YEAH...
Z
Z
Z
GET HIM UP.

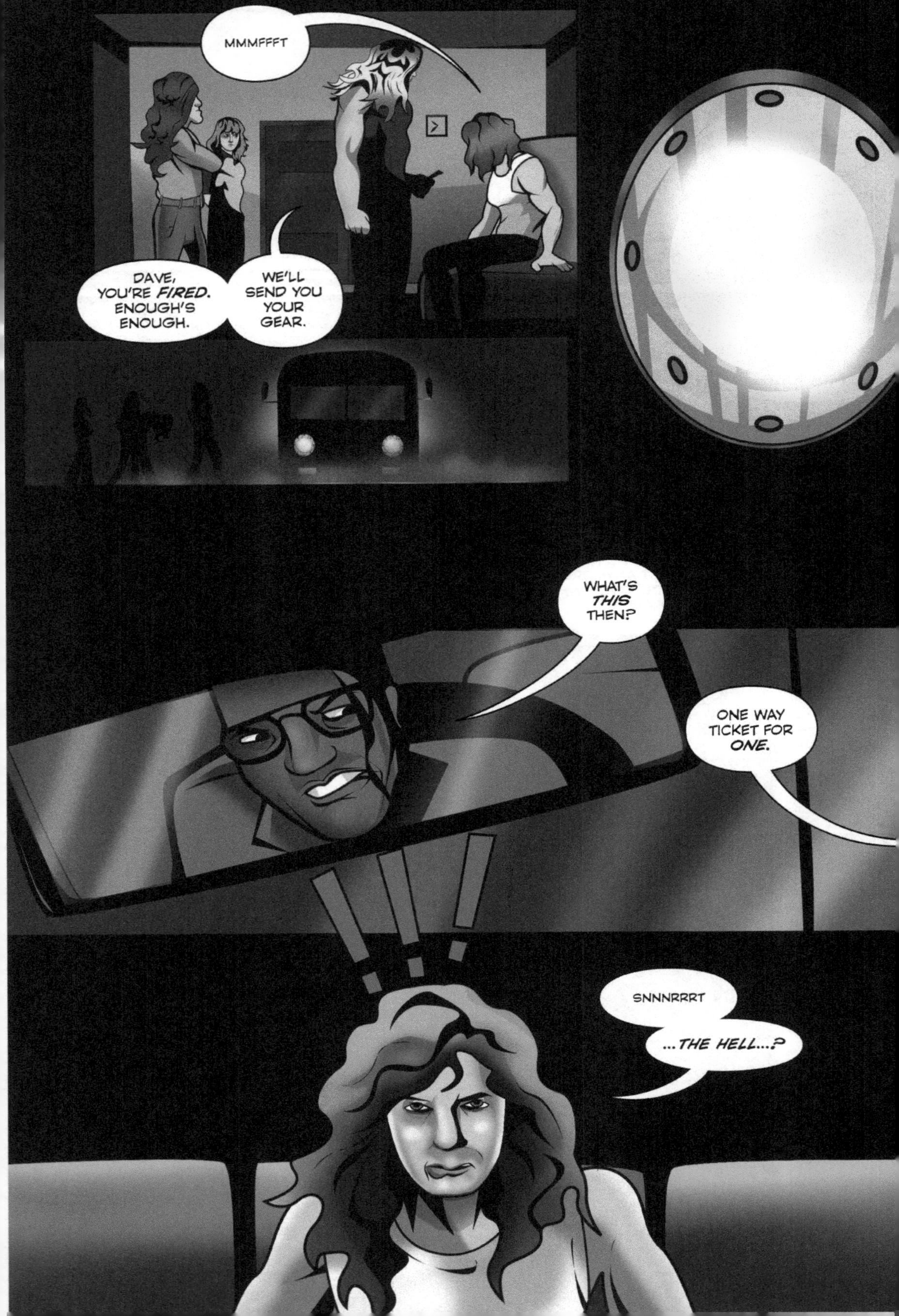
MMMFFFT
DAVE, YOU'RE *FIRED*. ENOUGH'S ENOUGH.
WE'LL SEND YOU YOUR GEAR.
WHAT'S *THIS* THEN?
ONE WAY TICKET FOR *ONE*.
!!!
SNNNRRRT
...*THE HELL*...?

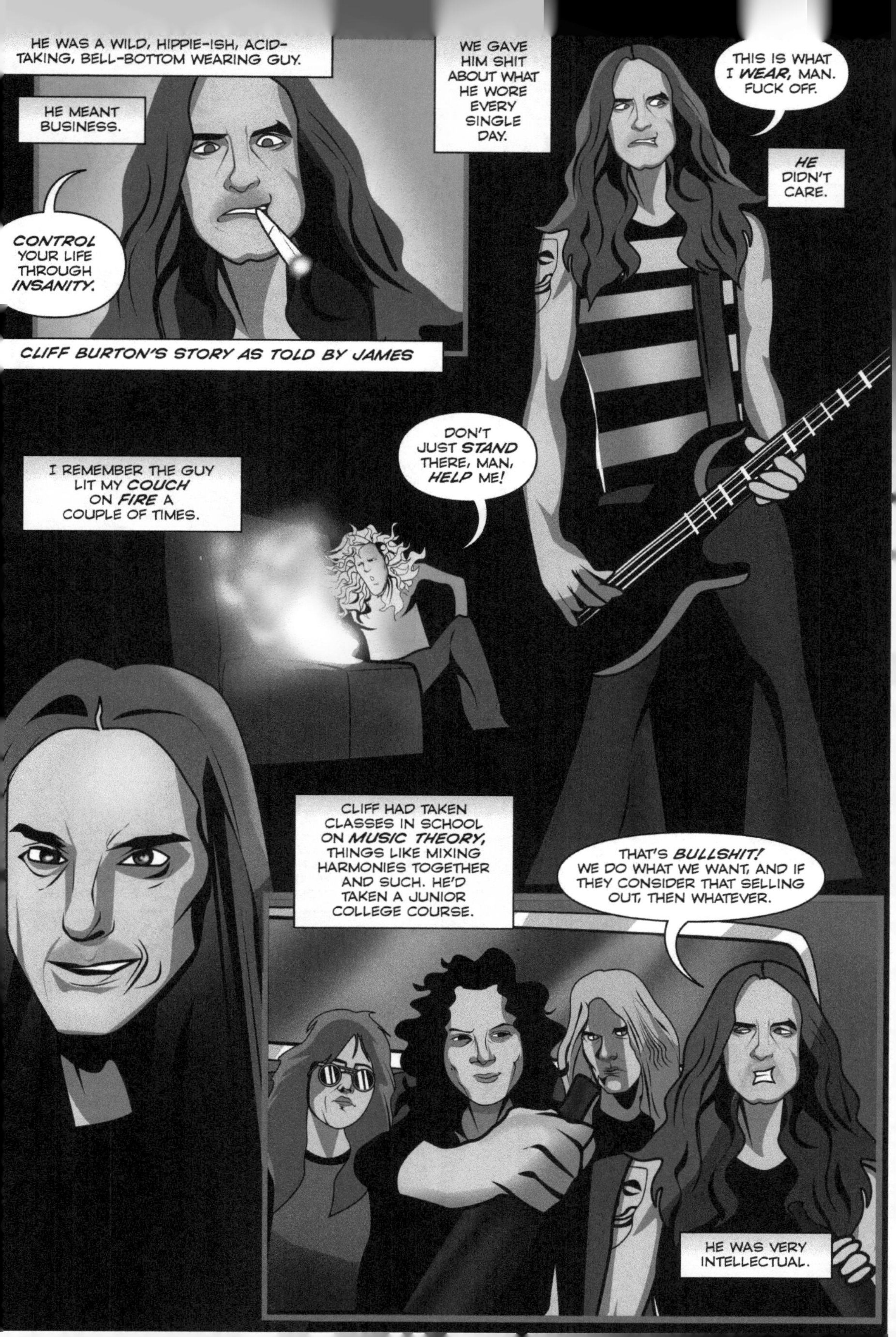
HE WAS A WILD, HIPPIE-ISH, ACID-TAKING, BELL-BOTTOM WEARING GUY.
HE MEANT BUSINESS.
CONTROL YOUR LIFE THROUGH INSANITY.
CLIFF BURTON'S STORY AS TOLD BY JAMES
WE GAVE HIM SHIT ABOUT WHAT HE WORE EVERY SINGLE DAY.
THIS IS WHAT I WEAR, MAN. FUCK OFF.
HE DIDN'T CARE.
I REMEMBER THE GUY LIT MY COUCH ON FIRE A COUPLE OF TIMES.
DON'T JUST STAND THERE, MAN, HELP ME!
CLIFF HAD TAKEN CLASSES IN SCHOOL ON MUSIC THEORY, THINGS LIKE MIXING HARMONIES TOGETHER AND SUCH. HE'D TAKEN A JUNIOR COLLEGE COURSE.
THAT'S BULLSHIT! WE DO WHAT WE WANT, AND IF THEY CONSIDER THAT SELLING OUT, THEN WHATEVER.
HE WAS VERY INTELLECTUAL.

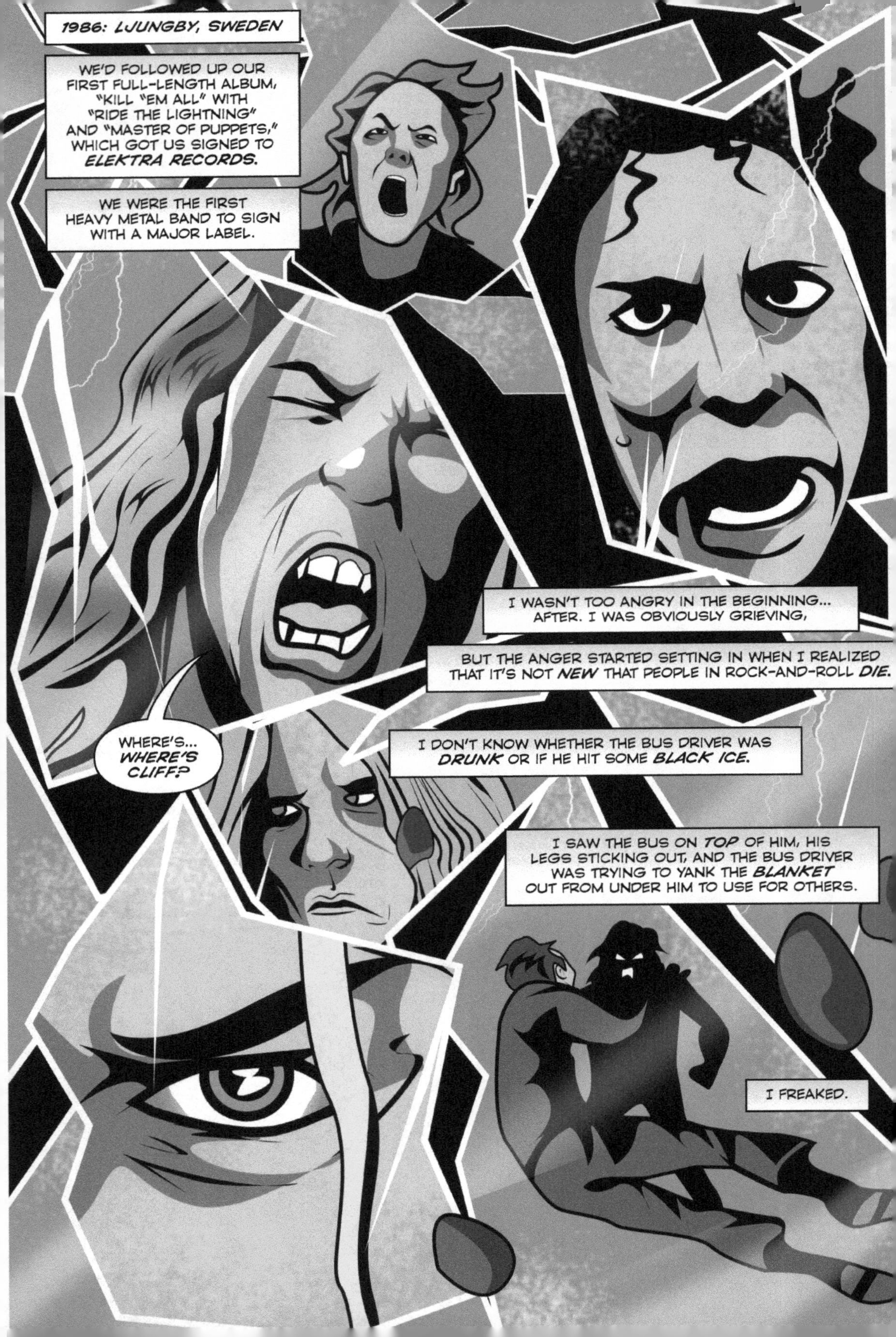

1986: LJUNGBY, SWEDEN
WE'D FOLLOWED UP OUR FIRST FULL-LENGTH ALBUM, "KILL 'EM ALL" WITH "RIDE THE LIGHTNING" AND "MASTER OF PUPPETS," WHICH GOT US SIGNED TO ELEKTRA RECORDS.
WE WERE THE FIRST HEAVY METAL BAND TO SIGN WITH A MAJOR LABEL.
I WASN'T TOO ANGRY IN THE BEGINNING... AFTER. I WAS OBVIOUSLY GRIEVING,
BUT THE ANGER STARTED SETTING IN WHEN I REALIZED THAT IT'S NOT NEW THAT PEOPLE IN ROCK-AND-ROLL DIE.
WHERE'S... WHERE'S CLIFF?
I DON'T KNOW WHETHER THE BUS DRIVER WAS DRUNK OR IF HE HIT SOME BLACK ICE.
I SAW THE BUS ON TOP OF HIM, HIS LEGS STICKING OUT, AND THE BUS DRIVER WAS TRYING TO YANK THE BLANKET OUT FROM UNDER HIM TO USE FOR OTHERS.
I FREAKED.

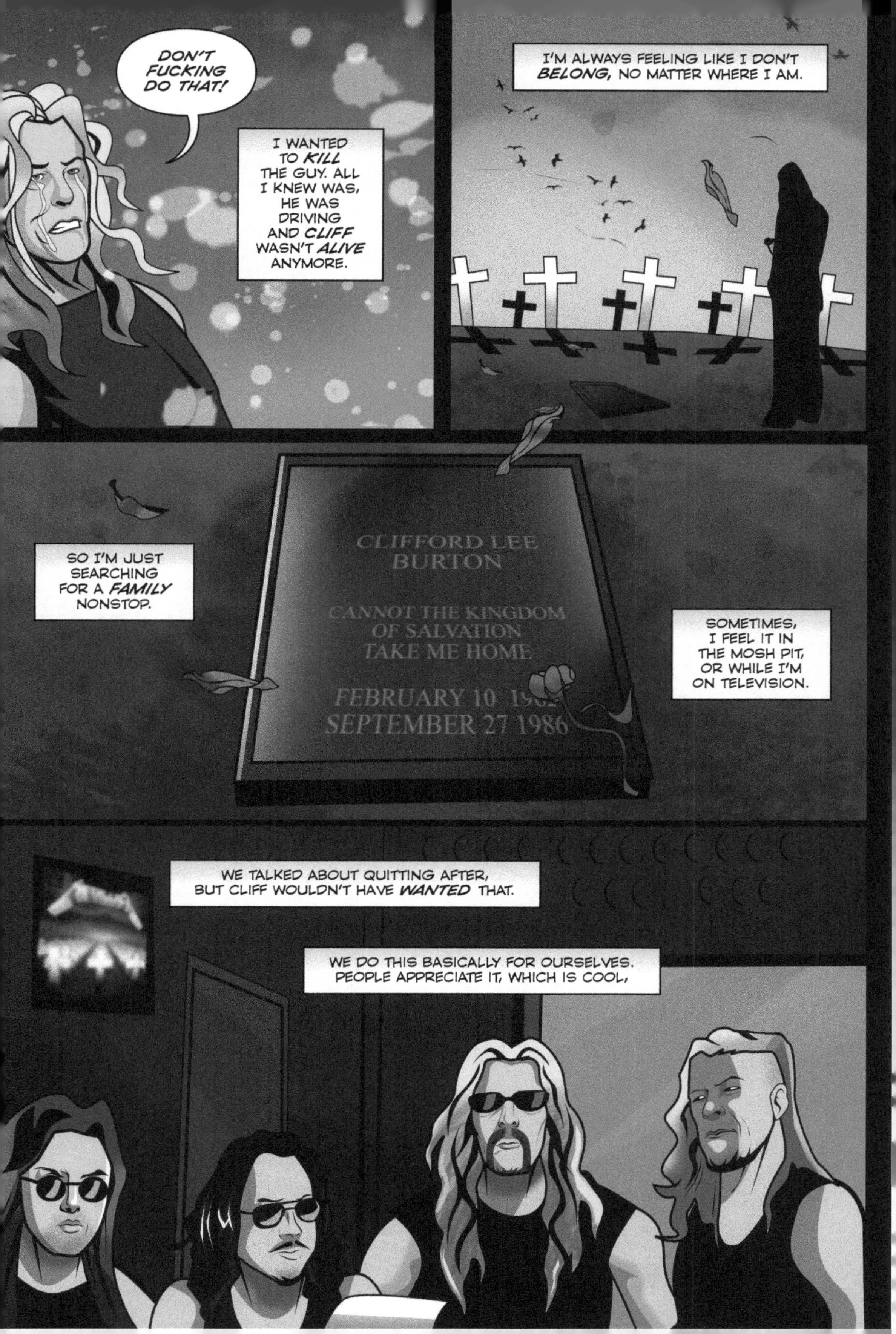
DON'T FUCKING DO THAT!
I WANTED TO KILL THE GUY. ALL I KNEW WAS, HE WAS DRIVING AND CLIFF WASN'T ALIVE ANYMORE.
I'M ALWAYS FEELING LIKE I DON'T BELONG, NO MATTER WHERE I AM.
SO I'M JUST SEARCHING FOR A FAMILY NONSTOP.
CLIFFORD LEE BURTON
CANNOT THE KINGDOM OF SALVATION TAKE ME HOME
SEPTEMBER 27 1986
SOMETIMES, I FEEL IT IN THE MOSH PIT, OR WHILE I'M ON TELEVISION.
WE TALKED ABOUT QUITTING AFTER, BUT CLIFF WOULDN'T HAVE WANTED THAT.
WE DO THIS BASICALLY FOR OURSELVES. PEOPLE APPRECIATE IT, WHICH IS COOL,

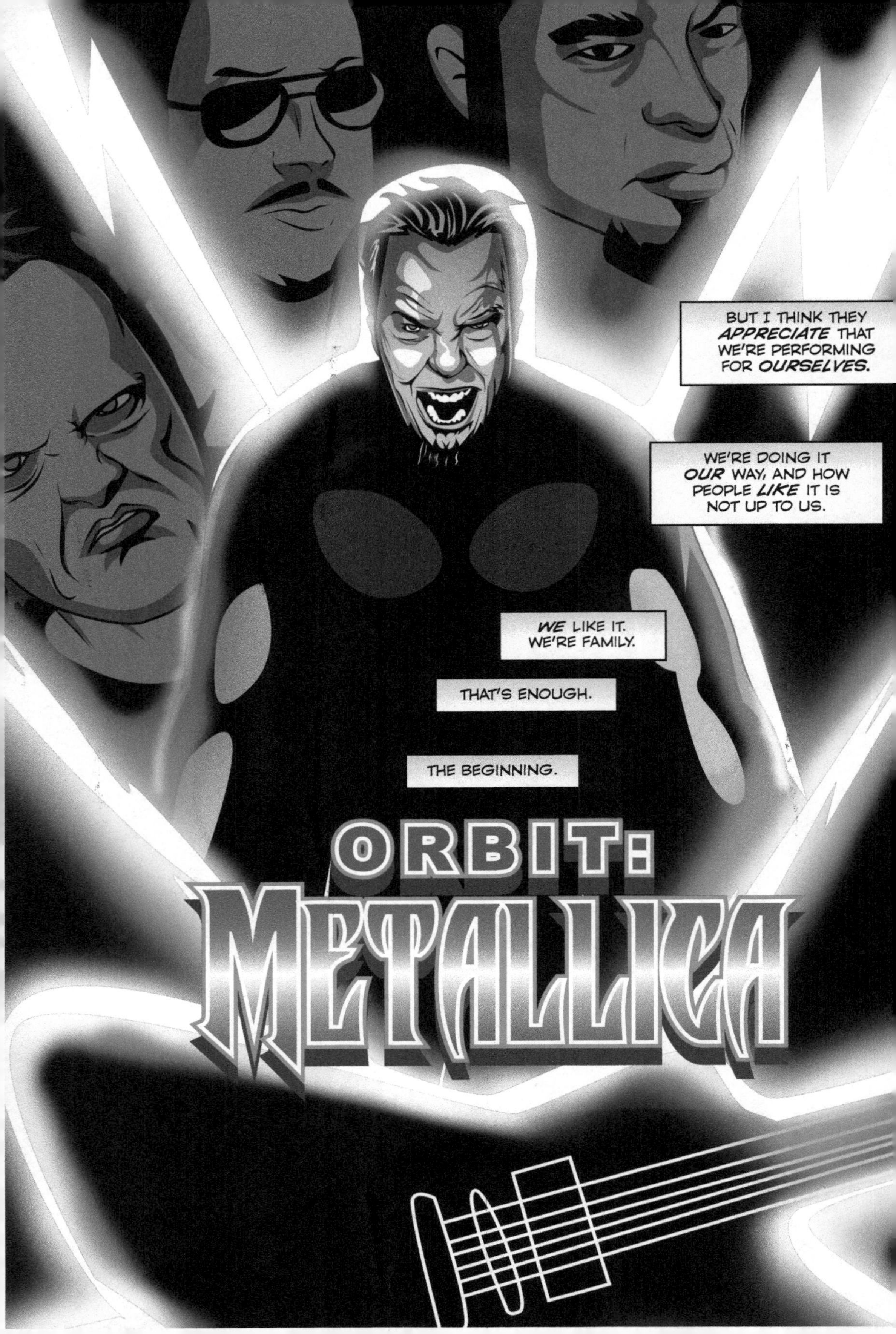
BUT I THINK THEY *APPRECIATE* THAT WE'RE PERFORMING FOR *OURSELVES.*
WE'RE DOING IT *OUR* WAY, AND HOW PEOPLE *LIKE* IT IS NOT UP TO US.
WE LIKE IT. WE'RE FAMILY.
THAT'S ENOUGH.
THE BEGINNING.
ORBIT:
METALLICA

Michael L. Frizell — Writer

Jayfri Hashim — Penciler

Jayfri Hashim — Colorist

Gary Scott Beatty — Letterer

David A. Frizell — Cover

Darren G. Davis
Publisher

Maggie Jessup
Publicity

Scott Kaufman
Entertainment Manager

Susan Ferris
Entertainment Manager

www.bluewaterprod.com

ORBIT AND CONTENTS ARE COPYRIGHT © AND ™ DARREN G. DAVIS. ALL RIGHTS RESERVED. BLUEWATER COMICS IS COPYRIGHT © AND ™ DARREN G. DAVIS. ALL RIGHTS RESERVED. ANY REPRODUCTION OF THIS MATERIAL IS STRICTLY PROHIBITED IN ANY MEDIA FORM OTHER THAN FOR PROMOTIONAL PURPOSES UNLESS DARREN G. DAVIS OR BLUEWATER COMICS GIVES WRITTEN CONSENT. PRINTED IN THE USA www.bluewaterprod.com

#ERASEHATE WITH THE MATTHEW SHEPARD FOUNDATION

With your donated dollars and volunteer hours, we work tirelessly to erase hate from every corner of America through our programs.

SPEAKING ENGAGEMENTS

Since Matt's death in 1998, Judy and Dennis have been determined to prevent others from similar tragedies. By sharing their story, they are able to carry on Matt's legacy.

HATE CRIMES REPORTING

Our work to improve reporting includes conducting trainings for law enforcement agencies, building relationships between community leaders and law enforcement, and developing policy reform in reporting practices.

LARAMIE PROJECT

MSF offers support to productions of The Laramie Project, which depicts the events leading up to and after Matt's murder. It remains one of the most performed plays in America.

MATTHEW'S PLACE

MatthewsPlace.com is a blog designed to provide young LGBTQ+ people with an outlet for their voices. From finance to health to love and dating, and everything in between, our writers contribute excellent material.

Erase Hate

Matthew Shepard Foundation
embracing diversity

CPSIA information can be obtained
at www.ICGtesting.com
Printed in the USA
BVHW011623150119
537878BV00008B/393/P